# Dalmatians

Characteristics, Personality and Temperament, Diet, Health, Where to Buy, Cost, Rescue and Adoption, Care and Grooming, Training, Breeding, and Much More Included!

By Lolly Brown

**Copyrights and Trademarks**

**Disclaimer and Legal Notice**

# Foreword

The Dalmatian is a very popular breed, known for its one-of-a-kind black and white spotted coat. The breed was made famous because of the Walt Disney movie adaptation of 101 Dalmatians. However, not a lot of people know the damage of that sudden fame to the Dalmatian breed. Many of the viewers of the film started buying Dalmatians and bringing them home without taking the time to educate themselves on the breed, which resulted to a high number of dogs being homeless or abandoned and most of them developing behavioral problems.

More than being an attractive and lovable dog, there is much more to the Dalmatians. So if you want to be a kind and responsible dog owner do the Dalmatians a favor and please learn as much as you can about the breed before even considering taking one home. As it happens, you're in luck because the book you are currently reading contains everything you'll need to know about having a Dalmatian as a pet so go on and turn the page!

# Table of Contents

# **Introduction**

When you hear the word Dalmatian, an image of a white dog with black spots most probably immediately pops up in your mind. Or maybe you're reminded of Pongo and Perdita and their absolutely adorable puppies from the movie 101 Dalmatians. The Dalmatian is one of the most popular breeds of dogs, but not everyone knows much about them other than what they watched in the film. And this led to a significant number of them being homeless or abandoned in shelters, and by then most of them had already developed behavioral problems due to lack of attention and proper training.

Bringing a dog home is a big responsibility and that responsibility begins when you're choosing the right breed for you. Choosing the right breed is like choosing a life partner because you're making a commitment and compatibility plays a big role. It's even more literal for dogs because they are the most loyal creatures in the world and they will live their entire lives as your companion. Ain't it a shame that they have shorter life spans than humans? Dogs can't choose their masters so make sure that you make the right choice. They deserve a good home where they will be loved and happy.

Dalmatians are not compatible with everyone. Like all dogs, they have special traits and needs. To find out if you're compatible with the Dalmatian, please continue reading this book to educate yourself on the breed. You will find all the information you need to know about becoming Dalmatian owner.

*Glossary of Dog Terms*

**AKC** – American Kennel Club, the largest purebred dog registry in the United States

**BAER** – Brainstem Auditory Evoked Response

**Balance** – A show term referring to all of the parts of the dog, both moving and standing, which produce a harmonious image

**Bite** – The position of the upper and lower teeth when the dog's jaws are closed; positions include level, undershot, scissors, or overshot

**Board** – To house, feed, and care for a dog for a fee

**Breed** – A domestic race of dogs having a common gene pool and characterized appearance/function

**Breed Standard** – A published document describing the look, movement, and behavior of the perfect specimen of a particular breed

**Coat** – The hair covering of a dog; some breeds have two coats, and outer coat and undercoat; also known as a double coat. Examples of breeds with double coats include German Shepherd, Siberian Husky, Akita, etc.

**Condition** – The health of the dog as shown by its skin, coat, behavior, and general appearance

**Cowhocks** – feet turned in or out

**Crate** – A container used to house and transport dogs; also called a cage or kennel

**Crossbreed (Hybrid)** – A dog having a sire and dam of two different breeds; cannot be registered with the AKC

**Dock** – To shorten the tail of a dog by surgically removing the end part of the tail

**Double Coat** – Having an outer weather-resistant coat and a soft, waterproof coat for warmth; see above

**Drop Ear** – An ear in which the tip of the ear folds over and hangs down; not prick or erect

**Fancier** – A person who is especially interested in a particular breed or dog sport

**Groom** – To brush, trim, comb or otherwise make a dog's coat neat in appearance

**Heel** – To command a dog to stay close by its owner's side

**Hypopigmentation** – Lack of pigmentation

**Inbreeding** – The breeding of two closely related dogs of one breed

**Kennel** – A building or enclosure where dogs are kept

**Litter** – A group of puppies born at one time

**Liver spots** – Brown spots

**Mate** – To breed a male and female dog

**Melanocytes** – cells that are vital for the normal functioning of the inner ear

**Neuter** – To castrate a male dog or spay a female dog

**Pads** – The tough, shock-absorbent skin on the bottom of a dog's foot

**Pedigree** – The written record of a dog's genealogy going back three generations or more

**Piebald** – A coloration on a dog consisting of patches of white and another color

**Puppy** – A dog under 12 months of age

**Purebred** – A dog whose sire and dam belong to the same breed and who are of unmixed descent

**Purine** – natural substance found in food that forms uric acid

**Ring tail** – tails that curve over the back

**Rubber curry brush** – molded rubber teeth to stimulate the production of natural oils to promote coat health

**Shedding** – The natural process whereby old hair falls off the dog's body as it is replaced by new hair growth.

**Smooth Coat** – Short hair that is close-lying

**Spay** – The surgery to remove a female dog's ovaries, rendering her incapable of breeding

**Trim** – To groom a dog's coat by plucking or clipping

**Wean** – The process through which puppies transition from subsisting on their mother's milk to eating solid food

**Whelping** – The act of birthing a litter of puppies

# Chapter One: Understanding Dalmatians

Dogs make wonderful pets if you find the perfect breed for you. If you think that the Dalmatian might be a good fit for you, take the time to learn everything you can. In this chapter you will find an overview of the Dalmatian breed including their history, physical characteristics and more. This information will help you make your decision. In the next chapter you will receive practical information about keeping Dalmatian dogs that you should also consider before deciding.

## Facts About Dalmatians

The Dalmatian is a very energetic, playful and athletic breed. They fall under the breed group of companions, which means that they need constant interaction with their owners. Leaving them leashed outside the house or in cages will develop aggressive and destructive behavior in them so if you don't have time and patience (both are required), then this breed isn't for you.

In terms of size, the female Dalmatian ranges from 20 – 22 inches (50 – 55 cm) while the male ranges from 22 – 24 inches (55 – 60 cm) – and the average weight for the breed is between 48 – 55 pounds. They have short white coats with black or liver spots. Some of them even have spots inside their mouths. These spots don't appear until about 4 weeks after they're born. For people who have allergies or are averse to sweeping, it is crucial for you to know that Dalmatians shed their short and fine hair every single day, all year round and there is no way to stop it. Their eye color could be brown or blue or both. Dalmatians that are well-bred have a regal and dignified stance.

Dalmatians are intelligent dogs but need proper training and lots of attention. Without proper training and if they're left alone too much, they become rebellious and destructive and in extreme cases they become uncontrollable. Dalmatians love to be around people and they thrive best when they share the same living space as their owners. They require plenty of mental stimulation and physical exercise. These two are a package deal because boredom will cause them to develop aggressive behavior and serious temperamental problems. For families with small children, it would be good to give the Dalmatian extra time and room for exercise to prevent the dog from becoming too exuberant that may result to accidentally hurting a child. Again, it needs to be emphasized that aspiring Dalmatian owners need to have a lot of patience, not only in training them but also with the little nuisances that come with having a dog. They have to be willing, prepared and equipped to train their dog. Furthermore, they need to be able to spend time with their dog. Workaholics, housewives who have their hands full, and other kinds of people who just don't have time to spare shouldn't even consider getting a Dalmatian. It could even be deduced that only dog lovers will have the adequate dedication to own this breed because they are the only ones who will truly enjoy spending time with them and not feel like it's a chore. When owning a dog, it is important to enjoy their company and make them feel loved because they are sensitive to human emotions and the rejection will most probably depress them.

In general, Dalmatians aren't noisy but when they're seriously lacking attention, they will keep barking until someone satisfies their craving for human interaction. They are clingy dogs. Scolding them will not alleviate the noise, and might even have the opposite effect. The Dalmatian is a headstrong dog and they can be very stubborn, especially if you don't teach them to respect you while they're still a puppy. Leniency will cause them to think that they are your master and not the other way around. To address the incessant barking, a simple pat will not be sufficient nor will a dog treat work because, more often than not, it is not food that they're asking for. They are asking for play time with you.

Dalmatians make dependable guard dogs because they have protective instincts and are very alert (provided that their hearing is intact). They can communicate warnings effectively.

Their lifespan usually ranges between 10 – 13 years. Like all breeds, they usually acquire health problems ranging from mild to serious and are caused by various factors. This will be discussed in a separate chapter.

## Summary of Dalmatian Facts

**Pedigree**: exact origins unknown, but the earliest sightings are claimed to be in Croatia

**AKC Group**: Companion, Utility, Sporting Group

**Breed Size**: medium to large

**Height**: 20 – 22 inches (50 – 55 cm) for females and 22 – 24 inches (55 – 60 cm) for males

**Weight**: 48 – 55 pounds

**Coat Length**: short

**Coat Texture**: fine and dense

**Shedding**: extreme, 365 days a year

**Color**: white with black or liver spots

**Eyes:** brown, blue or both

**Nose**: black, liver, blue, dark gray

**Ears**: drop ears; set high, tapering to a rounded tip

**Tail**: topline extension, never docked, tapers to the tip, carried with a slight upward curve

**Temperament**: energetic, lively, playful, alert, intelligent, clingy, outgoing

**Strangers**: may greet them with enthusiastic jumping or be politely reserved

**Children**: generally good with children but should be supervised around young and small children

**Other Dogs**: generally good with other dogs and other animals if properly trained and socialized

**Training**: intelligent and very trainable

**Exercise Needs**: has an endless supply of energy; can never have enough exercise so provide as much as possible, should not be less than an hour a day

**Health Conditions**: deafness, hypopigmentation, urination complications that lead to kidney and bladder stones

**Lifespan**: average 10 to 13 years

**Nickname:** Dal

## Dalmatian Breed History

The Dalmatians are an ancient breed that goes as far back as 2000 BC; hence, the exact origin of the Dalmatian breed is unknown. The breed is said to have traveled with gypsies, been sighted in Greek and Egyptian murals, and its first illustration and some very early records are found in Croatia. Incidentally, Croatia was formerly named Dalmatia, which is where the breed got its name. However, efforts to have the breed recognized as Croatian has been futile and they are still refused the patronage rights over the Dalmatians.

In addition to being companion dogs, they are also included in the group of utility and sporting dogs because they have great stamina and exceptional endurance. They are a very dynamic breed and have been known for many talents over the years. They were war sentinels, cart pullers, sheep herders, bird dogs, trail hounds, retrievers, and circus performers.

In England, they were bred to become coaching dogs. The U.S. version of this is the firehouse dog. They are similar functions, both based on the fact, which still remains today, that Dalmatians have a strong, natural affinity for horses. Coach dogs were used to clear paths for horse-drawn carriages and to ward off any threat or disturbance that may cause distress to the horses. They are very swift runners because they can run alongside the horses and they have graceful bounds and strides. Firehouse dogs were part of fire rescue squads and their main job was to accompany horses and keep them calm. Up to this day, firehouses use Dalmatians as their mascots.

# Chapter Two: Things to Know Before Getting a Dalmatian

Now that you're acquainted with the Dalmatian, more or less you already know if you're compatible with the breed. However, you also have to take into consideration the more practical aspects of owning a dog. In this chapter you will find licensing requirements, initial and monthly costs of dog ownership, and a summary of pros and cons for the breed. This chapter should help you further in making an informed decision on whether you are capable and ready to own a pet.

## Do You Need a License?

Before purchasing a Dalmatian dog, you should learn about local licensing requirements that may affect you. The licensing requirements for dog owners vary from one country to another so you may need to do a little bit of research on your own to determine whether you need a dog license or not. In the United States, there are no federal requirements for dog licensing – it is determined at the state level. While some states do not, most states require dog owners to license their dogs on an annual basis.

When you apply for a dog license you will have to submit proof that your dog has been given a rabies vaccine. Dog licenses in the United States cost about $25 (£16.25) per year and they can be renewed annually when you renew your dog's rabies vaccine. Even if your state doesn't require you to license your dog it is still a good idea because it will help someone to identify him if he gets lost so they can return him to you.

In the United Kingdom, licensing requirements for dog owners are a little bit different. The U.K. requires that all dog owners license their dogs and the license can be renewed every twelve months. The cost to license your dog in the U.K. is similar to the U.S. but you do not have to have your dog vaccinated against rabies. In fact, rabies does not exist in the U.K. because it was eradicated through careful control measures. If you travel with your dog to or from the U.K., you will have to obtain a special animal moving license and your dog may have to undergo a period of quarantine to make sure he doesn't carry disease into the country.

## Do Dalmatians Get Along with Other Pets?

If a Dalmatian is successfully trained and adequately socialized, he is generally very friendly towards all kinds of animals and he gets along well with other pets. However, if the owner fails to establish that he is the alpha and allows the dog to think that he is in charge, behavioral problems are guaranteed to arise, including but not limited to aggressive behavior towards other animals.

## How Many Dalmatians Should You Keep?

Definitely not a hundred and one. Dalmatians are needy and demanding and keeping them as a pet will be exhausting at times. These dogs don't like being neglected or ignored. Though they generally get along well with other pets, it is not advisable to get more than one unless you can give them equal time and attention. However, getting another breed that isn't competitive and territorial might be a good idea so that your dog will have unlimited access to play time and will secure his daily exercise regimen. Nevertheless, it is important to remember that a dog companion cannot be your replacement so you still need to fulfill your duties as your pet's master.

*How Much Does it Cost to Keep a Dalmatian?*

Most people who aspire to own a dog don't realize that the cost is more than just the purchase price itself. Owning pets mean including them in your budget because the expenses are as a regular as your grocery and utility bills. Spending on your Dalmatian will begin even before you take him home because you have to prepare for his arrival and you have to purchase a crate, toys, indoor gates or fences, and food bowls. The responsibility of being a dog owner also includes being able to provide for their needs so before you take one home make sure that you can keep up with the expenses. In this section you will receive an overview of the initial costs and monthly costs to keep a Dalmatian.

## Initial Costs

The initial costs for keeping a Dalmatian include those costs that you must cover before you can bring your dog home. Some of the initial costs you will need to cover include your dog's crate, food/water bowls, toys and accessories, microchipping, initial vaccinations, spay/neuter surgery and supplies for grooming and nail clipping – it also includes the cost of the dog itself. <u>You will find an overview of each of these costs as well as an estimate for each cost below</u>:

**Purchase Price** – The cost to purchase a Dalmatian can vary greatly depending where you find the dog. You can adopt a rescue Dalmatian for as little as $200 (£180) but purchasing a puppy, especially a purebred puppy from an AKC-registered breeder, could be much more costly. Dalmatian puppies can cost anywhere between $300 - $2000 (£210 – £1380). Just be cautious when buying from unregistered breeders and do a background check on their credibility. Make sure the puppy is completely healthy.

**Crate** – The Dalmatian is a medium to large breed so you'll have to buy a crate spacious enough. The average cost for a large dog crate is about $200 (£180) in most cases.

**Indoor Fences/Gates** – Aside from the crate, you'll need to create a space for your puppy that he can acknowledge as his own where you will set up his bed and toys. The average cost for these fences/gates is $100 (£70).

**Beds** –It is ideal to teach your puppy early on that there is a designated place for him to sleep. The average cost for beds is $100 (£70).

**Food/Water Bowls** – In addition to providing your Dalmatian with a crate to sleep in, you should also make sure he has a set of high-quality food and water bowls. The best materials for these are stainless steel because it is easy to clean and doesn't harbor bacteria. Choose bowls that are heavy so that the dog won't be able to push or tip it over and make a mess. The average cost for a quality set of stainless steel bowls is about $20 (£18).

**Toys** – Giving your Dalmatian plenty of toys to play with will help to keep him from chewing on things that are not toys – they can also be used to provide mental stimulation and enrichment. To start out, plan to buy an assortment of toys for your dog until you learn what kind he prefers. You may want to budget a cost of $50 (£45) for toys just to be sure you have enough to last through the puppy phase.

**Microchipping** – In the United States and United Kingdom there are no federal or state requirements saying that you have to have your dog microchipped, but it is a very good idea. Your Dalmatian could slip out of his collar on a walk or lose his ID tag. If someone finds him without identification, they can take him to a shelter to have his microchip scanned. A microchip is something that is implanted under your dog's skin and it carries a number that is linked to your contact information. The procedure takes just a few minutes to perform and it only costs about $30 (£19.50) in most cases.

**Initial Vaccinations** – During your dog's first year of life, he will require a number of different vaccinations. If you purchase your puppy from a reputable breeder, he might already have had a few but you'll still need more over the next few months as well as booster shots each year. You should budget about $50 (£32.50) for initial vaccinations just to be prepared.

**Spay/Neuter Surgery** – If you don't plan to breed your Dalmatian you should have him or her neutered or spayed before 6 months of age. The cost for this surgery will vary depending where you go and on the sex of your Dalmatian. If you go to a traditional veterinary surgeon, the cost for spay/neuter surgery could be very high but you can save money by going to a veterinary clinic. The average cost for neuter surgery is $50 to $100 (£32.50 - £65) and spay surgery costs about $100 to $200 (£65 - £130).

**Supplies/Accessories** – In addition to purchasing your Dalmatian's crate and food/water bowls, you should also purchase some basic grooming supplies (several brushes and a wide-toothed comb) as well as a leash and collar. The cost for these items will vary depending on the quality, but you should budget about $100 (£32.50) for these extra costs.

| Initial Costs for Dalmatians | | |
|---|---|---|
| **Cost** | **One Dog** | **Two Dogs** |
| Purchase Price | $200 - $2,000 (£180 - £1,800) | $400 - $4,000 (£360 - £3,600) |
| Crate | $200 (£180) | $400 (£360) |
| Fences/Gates | $100 (£70) | $100 (£70) |
| Food/Water Bowl | $20 (£18) | $40 (£36) |
| Toys | $50 (£45) | $100 (£90) |
| Microchipping | $30 (£19.50) | $60 (£39) |

| Vaccinations | $50 ($32.50) | $100 ($65) |
|---|---|---|
| Spay/Neuter | $50 to $200 (£32.50 - £130) | $100 to $400 (£65 - £260) |
| Accessories | $100 (£90) | $100 (£90) |
| **Total** | $800 to $2750 (£550 - £1900) | $1400 to $5300 (£968 – £3660) |

*Costs may vary depending on location
**U.K. prices based on an estimated exchange of $1 = £0.90

## Monthly Costs

The monthly costs for keeping a Dalmatian as a pet include those costs which recur on a monthly basis. The most important monthly cost for keeping a dog is, of course, food. In addition to food, however, you'll also need to think about things like annual license renewal, toy replacements, and veterinary exams. <u>You will find an overview of each of these costs as well as an estimate for each cost on below</u>:

**Food and Treats** – Feeding your Dalmatian a healthy diet is very important for his health and wellness. A high-quality diet for dogs is not cheap, so you should be prepared to spend around $35 (£31.50) on a large bag of high-quality dog food which will last you at least a month. You should also include a monthly budget of about $10 (£6.50) for treats.

**License Renewal** – The cost to license your Dalmatian will generally be about $25 (£16.25) and you can renew the license for the same price each year. License renewal cost divided over 12 months is about $2 (£1.30) per month.

**Veterinary Exams** – In order to keep your Dalmatian healthy you should take him to the veterinarian about every six months after he passes puppyhood. You might have to take him more often for the first 12 months to make sure he gets his vaccines on time. The average cost for a vet visit is about $40 (£26) so, if you have two visits per year, it averages to about $7 (£4.55) per month.

**Other Costs** – In addition to the monthly costs for your Dalmatian's food, license renewal, and vet visits there are also some other cost you might have to pay occasionally. These costs might include things like replacements for worn-out toys, a larger collar as your puppy grows, cleaning products, and more. You should budget about $15 (£9.75) per month for extra costs.

| Monthly Costs for Dalmatians | | |
|---|---|---|
| **Cost** | **One Dog** | **Two Dogs** |
| Food and Treats | $45 (£40.50) | $90 (£81) |
| License Renewal | $2 (£1.30) | $4 (£3.60) |
| Veterinary Exams | $7 (£4.55) | $14 (£12.60) |
| Other Costs | $15 (£9.75) | $30 (£19.50) |
| **Total** | $99 (£89) | $198 (£178) |

*Costs may vary depending on location
**U.K. prices based on an estimated exchange of $1 = £0.90

## What are the Pros and Cons of Dalmatians?

Bringing home a pet is a big decision to make because it is a big responsibility. It's another mouth to feed, another living being to take care of, raise and look after. You have to make sure that you are ready for the obligation and that you are equipped to handle it. So load up your arsenal with more information on the Dalmatian as a pet and read on to weigh the pros and cons of the breed. You will find a list of pros and cons for the Dalmatian dog breed listed on the following page:

## Pros for the Dalmatian Breed

- Has a great sense of humor and they will often try to make you laugh
- Great guard dogs because of their alertness and protective instincts
- Generally friendly with everyone they meet
- Very devoted and loyal companions, forms close bonds with family
- Generally do not bark excessively
- Makes a great family pet and companion animal, generally gets along with children
- Usually gets along with other dogs and household pets, including cats
- Intelligent and very trainable
- Easy to groom so you don't have to spend for it
- Generally clean with no doggy odor

## Cons for the Dalmatian Breed

- Serious health issues
- Demands constant attention and patience and lots of time that can sometimes be exhausting
- Willful and sometimes obstinate or manipulative, challenging their owners to prove that they are the authority

- Becomes destructive and aggressive when neglected, bored and left alone for long periods of time without physical and mental exercise
- They shed every single day of every year
- Rowdy and too exuberant that usually results to things or people knocked over or broken furniture
- Not suitable for apartments or small living spaces

# Chapter Three: Purchasing Dalmatians

If your heart and mind is now set on getting a Dalmatian, you can now go dog hunting. Be advised that for the Dalmatian breed the more superior choice is to bring home a puppy instead of a mature dog because with this breed establishing your authority and earning their respect is crucial in being able to train them. Even if the adult Dalmatian is already housetrained and socialized, you will have difficulty getting them to obey you because of their willful and headstrong trait. If your authority isn't established early on, they will not recognize it and they will keep challenging you. This chapter gives you useful information about finding a good Dalmatian breeder. You will also read about valuable tips for picking out a healthy Dalmatian puppy and for puppy-proofing your home.

## Where Can You Buy Dalmatians?

If you are sure that a Dalmatian is right for you, you need to start thinking about where you are going to get your new dog. Many people think that the best place to find a dog is at the pet store but, unfortunately, they are greatly mistaken. While the puppies at the pet store might look cute and cuddly, there is no way to know whether they are actually healthy or well-bred. Many pet stores get their puppies from puppy mills and they sell the puppies to unsuspecting dog lovers. Puppy mill puppies are often already sick by the time they make it to the pet store, often traveling across state lines to get there.

A puppy mill is a type of breeding facility that focuses on breeding and profit more than the health and wellbeing of the dogs. Puppy mills usually keep their dogs in squalid conditions, forcing them to bear litter after litter of puppies with little to no rest in between. Many of the breeders used in puppy mills are poorly bred themselves or unhealthy to begin with which just ensures that the puppies will have the same problems. The only time you should bring home a puppy from a pet store is if the store has a partnership with a local shelter and that is where they get their dogs. If the pet store can't tell you which breeder the puppies came from, or if they don't offer you any paperwork or registration for the puppy, it is likely that the puppy came from a puppy mill.

Rather than purchasing a Dalmatian puppy from a pet store, your best bet is to find a reputable Dalmatian breeder – preferably and AKC-registered breeder in the United States or a Kennel Club-registered breeder in the U.K. If you visit the website for either of these organizations you can find a list of breeders for all of the club-recognized breeds. You can also look for breeders on the website for other breed clubs like The Dalmatian Club of America or The British Dalmatian Club. Even if these organizations don't provide a list of breeders you may be able to speak with members to find information.

If you don't have your heart set on a Dalmatian puppy, you may consider adopting a rescue from a local shelter. There are many benefits associated with rescuing an adult dog. For one thing, adoption fees are generally under $200 (£180) which is much more affordable than the $800 to $1,200 (£720 to £1,080) fee to buy a puppy from a breeder. Plus, an adult dog will already be housetrained. As an added bonus, most shelters spay/neuter their dogs before adopting them out so you won't have to pay for the surgery yourself. Another benefit is that an adult dog has already surpassed the puppy stage so his personality is set – with a puppy you can never quite be sure how your puppy will turn out. You may be lucky enough to find a Dalmatian that doesn't have obedience issues.

If you are thinking about adopting Dalmatian, consider one of these breed-specific rescues:

**United States Rescues:**

**Dalmatian Rescue**

< http://www.dalmatianrescue.com/>

**Dalmatian Rescue of Illinois**

< http://www.dalrescueillinois.org/>

**Save the Dalmatians and Other Canine Rescue**

< http://www.savethedals.org/>

Adopt a Spot Dalmatian Rescue Inc.

< http://adoptaspotdalrescue.com/>

## United Kingdom Rescues:

### All Dalmatian Rescue

< http://www.deafdal.co.uk/rescue.htm>

### British Dalmatian Welfare

< http://www.dalmatianwelfare.co.uk/>

The Dog Rescue Pages

< http://www.dogpages.org.uk/>

### North of England Dalmatian Welfare

< http://northofenglanddalmatianwelfare.co.uk/>

**You can also find a list of Dalmatians in need of homes using the Dalmatian Rescue Network directory.**

< http://dalmatian.rescueme.org/>

*How to Choose a Reputable Dalmatian Breeder*

When you are ready to start looking for a Dalmatian puppy you may begin your search for a breeder online. A simple internet search will probably give you a variety of results but, if you want to find a reputable breeder, you may have to dig a little deeper. The Dalmatian Club of America is a great place to start. Compile a list of breeders from whatever sources you can and then take the time to go through each option to determine whether the breeder is reputable and responsible or not. You do not want to run the risk of purchasing a puppy from a hobby breeder or from someone who doesn't follow responsible breeding practices. If you aren't careful about where you get your Dalmatian puppy you could end up with a puppy that is already sick.

Once you have your list of breeders on hand you can go through them one-by-one to narrow down your options. <u>Go through the following steps to do so</u>:

- Visit the website for each breeder on your list (if they have one) and look for key information about the breeder's history and experience.
  - o Check for club registrations and a license, if applicable.
  - o If the website doesn't provide any information about the facilities or the breeder you are best just moving on.
- After ruling out some of the breeders, contact the remaining breeders on your list by phone
  - o Ask the breeder the following questions:
    - How old are the parents?
    - Can you provide me with the health clearances of the parents?
    - Why did you decide upon this particular breeding?
    - Can you tell me about the dogs in the 3 generation pedigree?
    - How did you raise the puppies? Have you started training and socializing?
    - Can you provide references from previous buyers?

- The answers to these questions must be along these lines:
  - The female dog must not be younger than 18 months and the male should not be younger than 12 months. Dogs must be given time to mature before being bred.
  - The breeder must be able to present you with a Canine Health Information Center number as an assurance that the parents were screened and deemed healthy and fit to be bred.
  - The answer should have been well-thought out and it should include a rational objective.
  - A good breeder will be able to give you a detailed account of the 3 generation pedigree without batting an eyelash because he knows it by heart and he is proud of it.
  - The breeder should have already started introducing the world to the puppy and should be able to teach you how to continue training and socialization.
  - A good breeder stays in touch with the owners to provide assistance so he should be able to give you references.

- o Expect a reputable breeder to ask you questions about yourself as well – a responsible breeder wants to make sure that his puppies go to good homes.
- Schedule an appointment to visit the facilities for the remaining breeders on your list after you've weeded a few more of them out.
  - o Ask for a tour of the facilities, including the place where the breeding stock is kept as well as the facilities housing the puppies.
  - o If things look unorganized or unclean, do not purchase from the breeder.
  - o Make sure the breeding stock is in good condition and that the puppies are all healthy-looking and active.
- Narrow down your list to a final few options and then interact with the puppies to make your decision.
  - o Make sure the breeder provides some kind of health guarantee and ask about any vaccinations the puppies may have already received.
- Put down a deposit, if needed, to reserve a puppy if they aren't ready to come home yet.

*Tips for Selecting a Healthy Dalmatian Puppy*

After you have narrowed down your options for breeders you then need to pick out your puppy. If you are a first-time dog owner, do not let yourself become caught up in the excitement of a new puppy – take the time to make a careful selection. If you rush the process you could end up with a puppy that isn't healthy or one whose personality isn't compatible with your family. <u>Follow the steps below to pick out your Dalmatian puppy</u>:

- Ask the breeder to give you a tour of the facilities, especially where the puppies are kept.
  - o Make sure the facilities where the puppies are housed are clean and sanitary – if there is evidence of diarrhea, do not purchase one of the puppies because they may already be sick.
- Take a few minutes to observe the litter as a whole, watching how the puppies interact with each other.
  - o The puppies should be active and playful, interacting with each other in a healthy way. If they seem overly exuberant and hyperactive, it is only an indication of the Dalmatian's personality and is perfectly normal.

- o Avoid puppies that appear to be lethargic and those that have difficulty moving – they are most probably sick. Dalmatians are never sluggish.
- Approach the litter and watch how the puppies react to you when you do.
  - o If the puppies appear frightened they may not be properly socialized and you do not want a puppy like that.
  - o Some of the puppies may be somewhat cautious, but most of them should be very friendly, curious and interested in you.
- Let the puppies approach you and give them time to sniff and explore you before you interact with them.
  - o Pet the puppies and encourage them to play with a toy, taking the opportunity to observe their personalities.
  - o Single out any of the puppies that you think might be a good fit and spend a little time with them.
- Pick up the puppy and hold him to see how he responds to human contact.
  - o The puppy should be exuberant and hyperactive. It shouldn't be frightened of you and it should enjoy being pet.
- Examine the puppy's body for signs of illness and injury

- The puppy should have clear, bright eyes with no discharge. The coat should be even and bright white, no patches of hair loss or discoloration.
- If you're looking at Dalmatian puppies that are less than 4 weeks old, don't expect them to have spots yet. The spots only appear generally 4 weeks onward after their birth.
- Ring tails are faults in this breed and tails should never be docked.
- The ears should be clean and clear with no discharge or inflammation.
- The puppy's stomach may be round but it shouldn't be distended or swollen.
- The puppy should be able to walk and run normally without any mobility problems.
- Narrow down your options and choose the puppy that you think is the best fit.

Once you've chosen your puppy, ask the breeder about the next steps. Do not take the puppy home if it isn't at least 8 weeks old and unless it has been fully weaned and eating solid food.

## *Puppy-Proofing Your Home*

After you've picked out your Dalmatian puppy you may still have to wait a few weeks until you can bring him home. During this time you should take steps to prepare your home, making it a safe place for your puppy. The process of making your home safe for your puppy is called "puppy proofing" and it involves removing or storing away anything and everything that could harm your puppy. It might help for you to crawl around the house on your hands and knees, viewing things from your puppy's perspective to find potential threats.

<u>On the following page you will find a list of things you should do when you are puppy-proofing your home</u>:

- Make sure your trash and recycling containers have a tight-fitting lid or store them in a cabinet.

- Put away all open food containers and keep them out of reach of your puppy.

- Store cleaning products and other hazardous chemicals in a locked cabinet or pantry where your puppy can't get them.

- Make sure electrical cords and blind pulls are wrapped up and placed out of your puppy's reach.

- Pick up any small objects or toys that could be a choking hazard if your puppy chews on them.

- Cover or drain any open bodies of water such as the toilet, and outdoor pond, etc.

- Store any medications and beauty products in the medicine cabinet out of your puppy's reach.

- Check your home for any plants that might be toxic to dogs and remove them or put them out of reach.

- Block off fire places, windows, and doors so your puppy can't get into trouble.

- Close off any stairwells and block the entry to rooms where you do not want your puppy to be.

# Chapter Four: Caring for Dalmatians

After learning about the practical aspects of keeping a Dalmatian as a pet, you can now move on to learning how to care for your dog and the tasks involved. This section talks about his habitat and exercise requirements, and will teach you how to prepare your home and make it an ideal environment for your puppy. It is vital for both you and your puppy that he has a space to call his own so that you can feel safe knowing that you have a way to keep him confined in your absence without always keeping him in a crate.

## Before bringing your Dalmatian home

You should ask yourself these questions first:

- **Do you have allergies?**
  Dalmatians shed a lot of hair.
- **Do you have young children?**
  Toddlers are no match for a Dalmatian's energy and strength.
- **Are you patient?**
  Owning dogs is like having a permanent two year old at home. And Dalmatians take a bit longer than most breeds to mature. They need gentle but firm training and physical punishment doesn't work on them.
- **Are you renting or living with your parents?**
  Make sure you get permission and approval before getting a large dog.
- **Do you have a yard or a venue for exercise?**
  Dalmatians need a lot of exercise.
- **Are you physically active and fit?**
  If you're lazy and prefer to lounge on the couch, don't get a Dalmatian.

For families, it would also be a good idea to sit down and ask all members if they are all on board with getting a dog. Once the decision is agreed upon, you can all discuss house rules and the distribution of tasks when caring for the dog (e.g. off-limits areas, feeding time, potty time, etc.) However, you should assign only one member of the family who will be the primary authority figure of the dog and will be in charge of housebreaking and training at all times.

## *Habitat and Exercise Requirements for Dalmatians*

The Dalmatian is a medium to large breed, and in addition to that, they can become very boisterous. Therefore, if you live in an apartment or a small, cramp and cluttered space, you will need to rethink your decision in getting this breed. Even if you are ready to part with some of your possessions when the dog unintentionally breaks them, it still wouldn't be fair to your dog to confine him in tight spaces. Spacious and uncluttered houses with yards or gardens are the ideal environment for a Dalmatian. They thrive best when they stay indoors with you. Do not leave your Dalmatian outside for long periods of time. Also, this breed isn't suited to living outdoors during the cold seasons.

As you should already know, the Dalmatian requires vigorous and extensive exercise every day (sometimes even multiple times a day). They love to run so any activity that will allow them to run will suffice. If you go jogging, always be conscious to lead him and not the other way around because it will give him the impression that he is in charge. The Dalmatians are made to run long distances so they have great stamina and endurance and don't get tired easily. However, during warmer temperatures, they will not show you signs of overheating so make sure you offer them hydration in regular intervals and have the good sense when to know that he's had enough. Also consider the weather when taking your dog out for exercise. If it's too hot, the pavement might hurt or damage his pads so you might want to opt for playing games in the yard instead.

To make your Dalmatian comfortable and to ensure that he feels at-home, you will need to provide him with certain things. A crate is one of the most important things you will need when you bring your new Dalmatian puppy home. Not only will it be a place for your puppy to sleep, but it will also be a place where you can confine him during the times when you are away from home or when you cannot keep a close eye on him. Your puppy will also need some other basic things like a water bowl, a food bowl, a collar, a leash, toys, and grooming supplies.

When shopping for food and water bowls, safety and sanitation are the top two considerations. Stainless steel is the best material to go with because it is easy to clean and resistant to bacteria. Ceramic is another good option. Heavy bowls are also a plus because the puppy will be unable to tip it over or push it across the floor which will save you from cleaning unnecessary mess. Avoid plastic food and water bowls because they can become scratched and the scratches may harbor bacteria. For your dog's collar and leash, choose one that is appropriate to his size. This may mean that you will purchase several collars and leashes while your puppy is still growing. You might also consider a harness – this will be helpful during leash training because it will improve your control over your puppy and it will distribute pressure across his back instead of putting it all on his throat.

Provide your Dalmatian puppy with an assortment of different toys and let him figure out which ones he likes. Having a variety of toys around the house is very important because you'll need to use them to redirect your puppy's natural chewing behavior as he learns what he is and is not allowed to chew on. As for grooming supplies, you'll need a rubber curry brush for daily brushing.

*Setting Up Your Puppy's Area*

Before you bring your Dalmatian puppy home, you should set up a particular area in your home for him to call his own. The ideal setup will include your puppy's crate, a comfy dog bed, his food and water bowls, and an assortment of toys. You can arrange all of these items in a small room that is easy to block off or you can use a puppy playpen to give your puppy some free space while still keeping him somewhat confined. It would be ideal to choose a room where most of the activity in the house happens so that your puppy won't feel isolated.

When you bring your puppy home you'll have to work with him a little bit to get him used to the crate. It is very important that you do this because you do not want your puppy to form a negative association with the crate. You want your puppy to learn that the crate is his own special place, a place where he can go to relax and take a nap if he wants to. If you use the crate as punishment, your puppy will not want to use it.

To get your puppy used to the crate, try tossing a few treats into it and let him go fish them out. Feeding your puppy his meals in the crate with the door open will be helpful as well. You can also incorporate the crate into your playtime, tossing toys into the crate or hiding treats under a blanket in the crate. As your puppy gets used to the crate you can start keeping him in it with the door closed for short periods of time, working your way up to longer periods. Just be sure to let your puppy outside before and after you confine him and never force him to stay in the crate for longer than he is physically capable of holding his bowels and his bladder.

# Chapter Five: Meeting Your Dalmatian's Nutritional Needs

If you want your dog to live a long and healthy life, you have to learn what and how to feed him. Like all living beings, dogs need proper nutrition and their needs are different from humans. So you'll have to take the time to learn the proper diet your dog needs. This chapter will tackle the nutritional needs of a Dalmatian and will help you in choosing high-quality dog food. You will also learn tips on feeding your puppy to ensure that you'll keep him healthy.

## The Nutritional Needs of Dalmatians

Like all mammals, dogs require a balance of protein, carbohydrate and fat in their diets – this is in addition to essential vitamins and minerals. It is important to understand, however, that your dog's nutritional needs are very different from your own. For Dalmatians, it is crucial to take into consideration a unique characteristic of the Dalmatian's digestive system. They are the only breed that lacks a particular enzyme that is needed in digesting food that is heavily dense in protein and their metabolism is sensitive to purine, which may both lead to kidney and urinary bladder stones if not properly monitored.

Therefore, aside from carbohydrates and fat, the special balanced diet for Dalmatians should still include protein but not heavily dense (e.g. organ meat) and should be low in purine. Avoid wet food because they are usually high in purine. Kibble is a good choice because it also satisfies the puppy's need to chew on something and will help keep his teeth healthy as well. Because Dalmatians are at high risk for urinary infections and stones, it is also important that you make sure he drinks plenty of water all the time so that he can flush the waste in order to prevent the buildup.

## How to Select a High-Quality Dog Food Brand

Shopping for dog food can be difficult for some dog owners simply because there are so many different options to choose from. If you walk into your local pet store you will see multiple aisles filled with bags of dog food from different brands and most brands offer a number of different formulas. So how do you choose a healthy dog food for your Dalmatian?

The best place to start when shopping for dog food is to read the dog food label. Pet food in the United States is loosely regulated by the American Association of Feed Control Officials (AAFCO) and they evaluate commercial dog food products according to their ability to meet the basic nutritional needs of dogs in various life stages. If the product meets these basic needs, the label will carry some kind of statement from AAFCO like this:

*"[Product Name] is formulated to meet the nutritional levels established by the AAFCO Dog Food nutrient profiles for [Life Stage]."*

If the dog food product you are looking at contains this statement you can move on to reading the ingredients list. Dog food labels are organized in descending order by volume. This means that the ingredients at the top of the list are used in higher quantities than the ingredients at the end of the list. This being the case, you want to see high-quality sources of animal protein at the beginning of the list. Things like fresh meat, poultry or fish are excellent ingredients but they contain about 80% water. After the product is cooked, the actual volume and protein content of the ingredient will be less. Meat meals (like chicken meal or salmon meal) have already been cooked down so they contain up to 300% more protein by weight than fresh meats. For Dalmatians, make sure that the protein source does not come from organ meat like liver.

In addition to high-quality animal proteins, you want to check the ingredients list for digestible carbohydrates and healthy fats. For dogs, digestible carbohydrates include things like brown rice and oatmeal, as long as they have been cooked properly. You can also look for gluten-free and grain-free options like sweet potato and tapioca. It is best to avoid products that are made with corn, wheat, or soy ingredients because they are low in nutritional value and may trigger food allergies in your dog.

In terms of fat, you want to see at least one animal source such as chicken fat or salmon oil. Plant-based fats like flaxseed and canola oil are not necessarily bad, but they are less biologically valuable for your dog. If they are accompanied by an animal source of fat, it is okay. Just make sure that the fats included in the recipe provide a blend of both omega-3 and omega-6 fatty acids. This will help to preserve the quality and condition of your Dalmatian dog's skin and coat.

In addition to checking the ingredients list for beneficial ingredients you should also know that there are certainly things you do NOT want to see listed. Avoid products made with low-quality fillers like corn gluten meal or rice bran – you should also avoid artificial colors, flavors, and preservatives. Some commonly used artificial preservatives are BHA and BHT. In most cases the label will tell you if natural preservatives are used.

## Tips for Feeding Your Dalmatian

Dalmatians were bred to run with horses and they are filled with a lot of excess energy all the time so they don't have problems with burning off their calories. Obesity is not a problem of this breed. They generally have an athletic and muscular body. For puppies, you'll want to feed them small amounts of kibble frequently in a day – about 3 to 4 times a day. For adults, they eat about 3 to 5 cups of kibble twice a day – usually in the morning and evening.

It would also be wise to schedule his meal time so that a routine is established. And please don't feed him after a strenuous exercise that may cause him to gobble up his food. It would be best to control his intake and watch over him as he eats because if he eats his food (or drinks) too fast it may cause his stomach to flip, which is a very serious and sometimes fatal medical condition known as Gastric dilation and volvulus.

### Dangerous Foods to Avoid

It might be tempting to give in to your dog when he is begging at the table, but certain "people foods" can actually be toxic for your dog. As a general rule, you should never feed your dog anything unless you are 100% sure that it is safe. <u>Below you will find a list of foods that can be toxic to dogs and should therefore be avoided</u>:

- Alcohol
- Apple seeds
- Avocado
- Cherry pits
- Chocolate
- Coffee
- Garlic
- Grapes/raisins
- Hops
- Macadamia nuts
- Mold
- Mushrooms

- Mustard seeds
- Onions/leeks
- Peach pits
- Potato leaves/stems
- Rhubarb leaves
- Tea
- Tomato leaves/stems
- Walnuts
- Xylitol
- Yeast dough

If your Dalmatian eats any of these foods, contact the Pet Poison Control hotline right away at (888) 426 – 4435.

# Chapter Six: Training Your Dalmatian

Now we arrive at perhaps the most challenging part of owning a dog: training. In having children, this is the equivalent of raising them. To have a harmonious life with your pet, it is imperative that you are able to instill good behavior in him. A Dalmatian is a fun, dependable and priceless companion to have when successfully trained. He will cheer you up and make you laugh, he will watch out for you and always keep you company. The Dalmatian is an intelligent breed and it won't be hard to teach them, but the difficulty is in getting them to follow and obey you because of their obstinate nature. In this chapter you will be taught how to housebreak and socialize your puppy. Tips for training and teaching tricks are also included in this section.

*Socializing Your New Dalmatian Puppy*

The first three months of life is when your Dalmatian puppy will be the most impressionable. This is when you need to socialize him because the experiences he has as a puppy will shape the way he interacts with the world as an adult. If you don't properly socialize your Dalmatian puppy then he could grow up to be a mal-adjusted adult who fears new experiences. Some Dalmatians even become snappy and aggressive around strangers when they are not properly socialized. Fortunately, socialization is very simple – all you have to do is make sure that your puppy has plenty of new experiences. <u>Below you will find a list of things you should expose your puppy to for properly socialization</u>:

- Introduce your puppy to friends in the comfort of your own home.

- Invite friends with dogs or puppies to come meet your Dalmatian (make sure everyone is vaccinated).

- Expose your puppy to people of different sizes, shapes, gender, and skin color.

- Introduce your puppy to children of different ages – just make sure they know how to handle the puppy safely.

- Take your puppy with you in the car when you run errands.

- Walk your puppy in as many places as possible so he is exposed to different surfaces and surroundings.

- Expose your puppy to water from hoses, sprinklers, showers, pools, etc.

- Make sure your puppy experiences loud noises such as fireworks, cars backfiring, loud music, thunder, etc.

- Introduce your puppy to various appliances and tools such as blenders, lawn mowers, vacuums, etc.

- Walk your puppy with different types of harnesses, collars, and leashes.

- Once he is old enough, take your puppy to the dog park to interact with other dogs.

*Positive Reinforcement for Obedience Training*

Training a dog is not as difficult as many people think – it all has to do with the rewards. Think about this – if you want someone do so something for you, you probably offer them something in return. The same concept is true for dog training – if you reward your dog for performing a particular behavior then he will be more likely to repeat it in the future. This is called positive reinforcement training and it is one of the simplest yet most effective training methods you can use as a dog owner.

The key to success with dog training is two-fold. For one thing, you need to make sure that your dog understands what it is you are asking him. If he doesn't know what a command means it doesn't matter how many times you say it, he won't respond correctly. In order to teach your dog what a command means you should give it and then guide him to perform the behavior. Once he does, immediately give him a treat and praise him – the sooner you reward after identifying the desired behavior, the faster your puppy will learn.

The second key to success in dog training is consistency. While your puppy is learning basic obedience commands you need to use the same commands each and every time and you need to be consistent in rewarding him. If you maintain consistency it should only take a few repetitions for your puppy to learn what you expect of him. You can then move on to another command and alternate between them to reinforce your puppy's understanding. Just be sure to keep your training sessions short – about 15 minutes – so your puppy doesn't get bored.

## Negative Consequences for Respect Training

For a well-mannered dog who will not only follow you when you ask him to do something but who will also obey you when you ask him to stop doing unwanted actions, you need to earn his respect. Therefore, positive reinforcement is not enough training because it doesn't teach your dog to respect you. When your dog is not in the mood for a treat, they will just opt not to listen to your command. As established in this book previously, Dalmatians are a stubborn breed and they love to challenge the authority of their leaders. As their leader, you cannot ever let them think that you are their follower or else you will have problems in getting them to listen and obey you. Hence, respect training is a must. You have to establish rules so he'll know that you're capable of being his leader. When he misbehaves, you have to tell him "no" or "stop". You have to be firm but gentle. Do not hurt your Dalmatian because corporal punishment doesn't work on them. The good news is that Dalmatians are generally people pleasers so when they are (gently but firmly) reprimanded, they will most likely not want to repeat the misbehavior.  Remember: consistency is the key to successful training.


## Crate Training - Housebreaking Your Puppy


In addition to obedience training, house training is very important for puppies. After all, you don't want to spend your dog's entire life following after him with a pooper scooper. The key to house training is to use your puppy's crate appropriately. When you are able to watch your puppy, keep him in the same room with you at all times and take him outdoors once every hour or so to give him a chance to do his business. Always lead him to a particular section of the yard and give him a command like "Go pee" so he learns what is expected of him when you take him to this area.

When you can't watch your puppy and overnight you should confine him to his crate. The crate should be just large enough for your puppy to stand up, sit down, turn around and lie down in. Keeping it this size will ensure that he views the crate as his den and he will be reluctant to soil it. Just make sure that you don't keep your puppy in the crate for longer than he is physically capable of holding his bladder. Always take your puppy out before putting him in the crate and immediately after releasing him.

If you give your puppy ample opportunity to do his business outdoors and you keep him confined to the crate when you can't watch him, housetraining should only take a few weeks. Again, consistency is key here so always reward and praise your puppy for doing his business outside so he learns to do it that way. If your puppy does have an accident, do not punish him because he will not understand – he won't associate the punishment with the crime so he will just learn to fear you instead.

## *Teaching Tricks and Playing Games*

The Dalmatian is a very fun dog to play with so you should take advantage of that trait by teaching him tricks and playing games as an alternative for his daily exercise. When teaching tricks, only positive reinforcement should be applied. Never punish the dog for not being able to do the trick.

**Fetch** – Teaching your dog how to fetch is probably the most useful trick for him to learn. You'll get to teach him words, when you're lazy to get something he could get it for you, and it's an enjoyable game for him to play as an alternative for exercise. You should start with items that will excite him like a ball, a chewtoy or a bone. Make sure to properly and repeatedly label the item you are asking him to retrieve before throwing it and once he returns it, give him a reward. When his vocabulary expands, you can start making a game out of it by asking him to identify the item among a lot of other objects in the same place. Whenever he gets it right, it would be a good idea to increase the prize for motivation.

**Go to** – This is also a good trick for discipline that could be used for teaching him how to go to bed or outside to relieve his bladder or bowels. Much like the command fetch, you only have to point to the place and properly and repeatedly identify it. When he gets it right, give a reward.

**Hug** – Your Dalmatian would enjoy this immensely as he is naturally bouncy. It would also be a way to teach him how to greet people in a poised way. Upon arriving home, instruct him to sit down and stay and greet him formally. When you're ready to ask for a hug, open your arms wide and slap your chest like a gorilla. Then instruct him again to sit down. The hug will be reward enough for his polite and well-mannered greeting.

# Chapter Seven: Grooming Your Dalmatian Properly

Grooming Dalmatians is the easiest part of owning them. Because they have short coats, grooming them is a no-fuss task. Probably the only problem you will encounter when grooming them is getting wet when giving them a bath because they are not known to stay still under any circumstances. So if you want to have some fun instead of stressing out on getting wet, wear your swim suits and get ready to splash around.

Read on to learn how to clean your dog's ears, brush their teeth and trim their nails.

## *Recommended Tools to Have on Hand*

If you plan to groom your Dalmatian yourself you will need certain tools and supplies. Even if you choose to have your dog professionally groomed, you should still have some supplies available for daily brushing and occasional bathing. <u>You will find a list of several recommended grooming tools and supplies below</u>:

- Rubber curry brush
- Dog-friendly shampoo
- Nail clippers
- Dog-friendly ear cleaning solution
- Dog toothbrush
- Dog-friendly toothpaste

## *Tips for Bathing and Grooming Dalmatians*

If you know your Dalmatian well enough, common sense would tell you that it would be better to give him a bath outside in the yard so you don't have to clean any mess that he'll otherwise leave in your bathroom. When giving your dog a bath, the only important thing to remember is to avoid getting water inside his ears as this might lead to an infection. Lather his body generously with shampoo and wash with water. Tie him on a leash but keep him company while he dries off. Maybe you can toss a ball back and forth while waiting. When he's dry use a rubber curry brush to remove dead hair and to keep his coat shiny.

## Other Grooming Tasks

In addition to brushing and bathing your Dalmatian, you also need to engage in some other grooming tasks including trimming your dog's nails, cleaning his ears, and brushing his teeth. <u>You will find an overview of each of these grooming tasks below</u>:

### Trimming Your Dog's Nails

Your dog's nails grow in the same way that your own nails grow so they need to be trimmed occasionally. Most dog owners find that trimming their dog's nails once a week or twice a month is sufficient. Before you trim your Dalmatian's nails for the first time you should have your veterinarian or a professional groomer show you how to do it. A dog's nail contains a quick – the blood vessel that supplies blood to the nail – and if you cut the nail too short you could sever it. A severed quick will cause your dog pain and it will bleed profusely. The best way to avoid cutting your dog's nails too short is to just trim the sharp tip.

**Cleaning Your Dog's Ears**

The Dalmatian has drop ears which means that they hang down on either side of the dog's head. If the dog's ears get wet it creates an environment that is beneficial for infection-causing bacteria. Keeping your dog's ears clean and dry is the key to preventing infections. If you have to clean your dog's ears, use a dog ear cleaning solution and squeeze a few drops into the ear canal. Then, massage the base of your dog's ears to distribute the solution then wipe it away using a clean cotton ball.

**Brushing Your Dog's Teeth**

Many dog owners neglect their dog's dental health which is a serious mistake. You should brush your dog's teeth with a dog-friendly toothbrush and dog toothpaste to preserve his dental health. Feeing your dog dental treats and giving him hard rubber toys can also help to maintain his dental health.

# Chapter Eight: Breeding Dalmatians

Ideally, breeding dogs should be a decision that was reached through organized reasoning, rational objectives and thorough research. It shouldn't be an impulsive decision or an accidental event. Breeding dogs is an even more daunting responsibility and task compared to merely owning them. If you are after the money, don't do it. You will be lucky just to break even. It costs more than its worth. If you want to have more dogs of the same breed, don't do it. Just purchase another one. It's much more trouble than its worth. If you are a rookie dog owner, don't do it. You are not ready for the job. The only acceptable reason for breeding is if you honestly hold facts and evidence that your dog is special enough to contribute an improvement to its breed. If this is your reason, then go ahead and read on about breeding your Dalmatian dog.

## Basic Dog Breeding Information

Before you decide whether or not to breed your Dalmatian, you should take the time to learn the basics about dog breeding in general. If you do not want to breed your dog, the ASPCA recommends having him neutered or her spayed before the age of 6 months. For female dogs, six months is around the time the dog experiences her first heat. Heat is just another name for the estrus cycle in dogs and it generally lasts for about 14 to 21 days. The frequency of heat may vary slightly from one dog to another but it generally occurs twice a year. When your female dog goes into heat, this is when she is capable of becoming pregnant.

If you do plan to breed your Dalmatian, it is important that you wait until she reaches sexual maturity. Your dog may be full-size by the time she reaches one year of age, but most Dalmatian breeders recommend waiting until she is two years old to breed her. Not only does this ensure that the dog is mature enough to physically carry and bear a litter, but it also provides enough time for any serious health problems to develop. If the dog does display signs of congenital health problems, she should not be bred for fear of passing them on. Preferably, your dog should only be bred every other year because if she conceives and gives birth consecutively within a short span of time it may cause problems in her reproductive system.

Once you've made sure that you have chosen the ideal breeding pair you can start to think about the details of heat and breeding. When a female dog goes into heat there are a few common signs you can look for. The first sign of heat is swelling of the vulva – this may be accompanied by a bloody discharge. Over the course of the heat cycle the discharge lightens in color and becomes more watery. By the 10th day of the cycle the discharge is light pink – this is when she begins to ovulate and it is when she is most fertile. If you plan to breed your Dalmatian, this is when you want to introduce her to the male dog. If she isn't receptive to the male's advances, wait a day or two before trying again.

A dog is technically capable of conceiving at any point during the heat cycle because the male's sperm can survive in her reproductive tract for up to 5 days. If you don't plan to breed your Dalmatian, you need to keep her locked away while she is in heat. A male dog can smell a female dog in heat from several miles away and an intact male dog will go to great lengths to breed. Never take a female dog in heat to the dog park and be very careful about taking her outside at all. Do not leave her unattended in your backyard because a stray dog could get in and breed with her.

If you want to breed your Dalmatian, you will need to keep track of her estrus cycle so you know when to breed her. It generally takes a few years for a dog's cycle to become regular. Keep track of your dog's cycle on a calendar so you know when to breed her. Tracking her cycle and making note of when you introduce her to the male dog will help you predict the due date for the puppies. Once you do start breeding your dog, be sure to skip at least one heat cycle between litters – ideally, you should give your dog a year to rest between litters.

## Breeding Tips and Raising Puppies

After the male dog fertilizes the egg inside the female's body, the female will go through the gestation period during which the puppies start to develop inside her womb. The gestation period for Dalmatian dogs lasts for anywhere from 60 to 65 days with the average being 63. However, you won't be able to actually tell that your dog is pregnant until after the third week. By the 25th day of pregnancy it is safe for a vet to perform an ultrasound and by day 28 he should be able to feel the puppies by palpating the female's abdomen. At the six week mark an x-ray can be performed to check the size of the litter. The average litter size for Dalmatians is between 6 and 9 puppies, though occasionally there are really large broods and the record so far is 18 puppies.

While the puppies are growing inside your female dog's belly you need to take careful care of her. You don't need to feed your dog any extra until the fourth or fifth week of pregnancy when she really starts to gain weight. Make sure to provide your dog with a healthy diet and keep up with regular vet appointments to make sure the pregnancy is progressing well. Once you reach the fifth week of pregnancy you can increase your dog's daily rations in proportion to her weight gain.

After eight weeks of gestation you should start to get ready for your Dalmatian to give birth – in dogs, this is called whelping. You should provide your dog with a clean, safe, and quiet place to give birth such as a large box in a dimly lit room. Line the box with old towels or newspapers for easy cleanup after the birth and make sure your dog has access to the box at all times. As she nears her due date she will start spending more and more time in the box.

When your Dalmatian is ready to give birth her internal temperature will decrease slightly. If you want to predict when the puppies will be born you can start taking her internal temperature once a day during the last week of gestation. When the dog's body temperature drops from

100°F to 102°F (37.7°C to 38.8°C to about 98°F (36.6°C), labor is likely to begin very soon. At this point your dog will display obvious signs of discomfort such as pacing, panting, or changing positions. Just let her do her own thing but keep an eye on her in case of complications.

During the early stages of labor, your Dalmatian will experience contractions about 10 minutes apart. If she has contractions for more than 2 hours without giving birth, bring her to the vet immediately. Once your Dalmatian starts whelping, she will whelp one puppy about every thirty minutes. After every puppy is born, she will clean it with her tongue – this will also help stimulate the puppy to start breathing on its own. After all of the puppies have been born, the mother will expel the afterbirth and the puppies will begin nursing.

It is essential that the puppies start nursing as soon as possible after whelping so that they get the colostrum. The colostrum is the first milk a mother produces and it is loaded with nutrients as well as antibodies that will protect the puppies while their own immune systems continue developing. The puppies will generally start nursing on their own or the mother will encourage them. After the puppies nurse for a little while you should make sure that your mother dog eats something as well.

When they are first born, Dalmatian puppies are immaculately white and spotless. Their spots will only start appearing on their 4th week. They only weigh about .75 – 2 pounds and they will continue growing over the next several months until they zone in on their adult size. It is a good idea to weigh the puppies once a week or so to make sure they are growing at a healthy rate. When Dalmatian puppies are born they will have some very fine hair but it isn't enough to keep them warm – your mother dog will help with that. It is also very important to place the puppies in a warm place or under a light. The puppies will be born with their eyes and ears closed but they will start to open around the second or third week following birth.

Your Dalmatian puppies will be heavily dependent on their mother for the first few weeks of life until they start becoming more mobile. Around 5 to 6 weeks of age you should start offering your puppies small amounts of solid food soaked in broth or water to start the weaning process. Over the next few weeks the puppies will start to nurse less and eat more solid food. Around 8 weeks of age they should be completely weaned – this is when they are ready to be separated from their mother.

# Chapter Nine: Tips for Showing Your Dalmatian

Historically, Dalmatians were once used as circus dogs. This breed is not shy or averse to the spotlight so when properly trained, they could also be bred to be great show dogs. One of the joys of owning a pure-breed dog is having the pride to show them off. But before you get ahead of yourself, you should check if your Dalmatian has all the requirements of AKC to become a show dog. This chapter provides a summary of the standards of the AKC for a Dalmatian and how to prepare your dog for a show.

## *Dalmatian Breed Standard*

The AKC breed standard for the Dalmatian breed provides guidelines for both breeding and showing. AKC-registered breeders must select dogs that adhere to the standards of the breed and all Dalmatian owners who seek to show their dogs at AKC shows must compare them to the official breed standard as well. <u>Below you will find an overview of the breed standard for the American Dalmatian breed</u>:

## General Appearance and Temperament

The Dalmatian is a medium to large dog with distinct spots, poised and muscular, swift and agile, capable of great speed and endurance, and wears an intelligent expression. The breed has a stable and outgoing temperament with no suggestion of shyness.

## Head and Neck

The head is well-proportioned and in balance with the rest of the dog. The neck is arched, sufficiently long, free from throatiness and smoothly connects to the shoulders. The topline is smooth. The eyes are set moderately apart and well into the skull. They are somewhat round and medium in size, brown or blue or a combination of both in color. The ears are set high and close to the head, thin and fine in texture, wide at the base and gradually tapering to the tip. The muzzle is powerful, smoothly connected to the cheeks, parallel and about equal in length to the skull, and a scissors bite. The nose is black for black-spotted and brown for liver-spotted.

## Body and Tail

The chest is deep and ample. The ribs are well sprung, gradually curving into a moderate tuck up. The back is level and strong. The tail is never docked and is a natural extension of the topline – it is carried with a slight upward curve. The flanks narrow through short, muscular and slightly arched loins.

## Legs and Feet

The forelegs are straight, strong and sturdy. The hindquarters are powerful and well-muscled, parallel to each other from the point of the hock to the heel of the pad. The hocks are well let down. Feet are round and compact with thick elastic pads and arched toes.

## Coat and Texture

The coat is short and fine and sleek.

## Color

The dominant color should be white with black or liver spots. Spots should be mostly round, distinct and ideally shouldn't be overlapping. They should be distributed evenly to give a pleasing appearance. The size varies – it could be as small as a dime or as big as a half dollar. Spots are usually larger on the body than other parts.

## Size

The ideal height is 19 – 23 inches. The length of the body should be proportioned to its height.

## Gait

The gait should be balanced, steady, effortless and powerful. They should have a certain dignified grace and agility that doesn't waver because of their endurance.

## Disqualifications

- Any dog under or over the standard size
- Shyness or timidity
- Abnormal position of eyelids or eyelashes
- Incomplete pigmentation of the eye rims and nose
- Underbite or overbite
- Ring tails and low-set tails
- Cowhocks
- Spots that are neither black nor liver
- Patches – solid mass of black or liver hair with no white
- Deafness

*Preparing Your Dalmatian for Show*

Once you've determined that your Dalmatian is a good representation of the official breed standard, then you can think about entering him in a dog show. Dog shows occur all year-round in many different locations so check the AKC or Kennel Club website for shows in your area. Remember, the rules for each show will be different so make sure to do your research so that you and your Dalmatian are properly prepared for the show.

On the following page you will find a list of some general and specific recommendations to follow during show prep:

- Make sure that your Dalmatian is properly socialized to be in an environment with many other dogs and people.

- Ensure that your Dalmatian is completely housetrained and able to hold his bladder for at least several hours.

- Solidify your dog's grasp of basic obedience – he should listen and follow basic commands.

- Do some research to learn the requirements for specific shows before you choose one – make sure your dog meets all the requirements for registration.

- Make sure that your Dalmatian is caught up on his vaccinations (especially Bordetella since he will be around other dogs) and have your vet clear his overall health for show.

- Have your dog groomed about a week before the show and then take the necessary steps to keep his coat clean and in good condition.

In addition to making sure that your Dalmatian meets the requirements for the show and is a good representation of the AKC breed standard, you should also pack a bag of supplies that you will need on the day of show. <u>Below you will find a list of helpful things to include in your dog show supply pack</u>:

- Registration information
- Dog crate or exercise pen
- Grooming table and grooming supplies
- Food and treats
- Food and water bowls
- Trash bags
- Medication (if needed)
- Change of clothes
- Food/water for self
- Paper towels or rags

- Toys for the dog

If you want to show your Dalmatian but you don't want to jump immediately into an AKC show, you may be able to find some local dog shows in your area. Local shows may be put on by a branch of a national Dalmatian breed club and they can be a great place to learn and to connect with other Dalmatian owners.

# Chapter Ten: Keeping Your Dog Healthy

Another one of the responsibilities of owning a dog is ensuring that you keep him healthy. This doesn't only involve feeding him properly but also taking the necessary precautions against sicknesses that may befall him. You have to schedule regular check-ups with his veterinarian to keep track of his overall health. It would also be prudent to learn the diseases that are high at risk for your Dalmatian so you can prevent them by avoiding the possible causes. This is an important chapter to read if you want your pet to live a long and healthy life because it will give you an overview of the common health afflictions for the Dalmatian as well as the basic vaccine timetable that your dog needs.

## Common Health Problems Affecting Dalmatian

A reality we all have to live by is that none of us is exempted from getting sick. Yes, Dalmatians are a fairly healthy breed but like any other living being they can develop illnesses whether mild or severe.

In this section, you will receive information about the common health problems that could affect your Dalmatian.

Some of the common conditions affecting Dalmatians include:

- Allergies
- Hereditary deafness
- Urolithiasis or Hyperuricemia
- Laryngeal paralysis

**Allergies**

Just like humans, dogs can develop allergic reactions to a number of different things. An allergy develops when the dog's immune system identifies a substance as pathogenic, or dangerous, and it launches an attack. The three main types of allergens can be inhaled, ingested, or taken into the body through skin contact. Dogs can develop allergies at any time and some breeds are more prone to allergies than others such as Cocker Spaniels, Terriers, Retrievers, Setters, and brachycephalic breeds like Pugs and

Bulldogs.

Common symptoms of allergies in dogs include red or itchy skin, runny eyes, increased scratching, ear infections, sneezing, vomiting, diarrhea, and swollen paws. Some common allergens for dogs include smoke, pollen, mold, dust, dander, feathers, fleas, medications, cleaning products, certain fabrics, and certain foods. Surprisingly, food allergies tend to produce skin-related symptoms like itching and scratching rather than digestive symptoms. Chronic ear infections are also a common sign of food allergies in dogs. The best treatment for allergies is avoiding contact with the allergen. For some environmental allergens, your vet might prescribe antihistamines or your vet might give your dog an injection to protect him.

**Hereditary Deafness**

All Dalmatian bloodlines carry the deaf gene. About 8% are born completely deaf and 22% are born with hearing in only one ear. In dogs that carry these genes, the blood supply to the inner ear degenerates sometime around the three- to four-week mark. The result is complete deafness in one or both ears and it is permanent. All puppies must be BAER tested to find out if they can hear or not because it is the only accurate way to find out: it is not that easy to detect deafness in dogs since they are sensitive and can rely on vibrations rather than sound. The test can be administered any time after 5 weeks of age.

The condition is common among piebald breeds and those that have the tendency for light pigmentation due to the absence of mature melanocytes in the inner ear. Dalmatians that are born with large patches are less prone to deafness but you have to take note that patches are a disqualifying factor in the breed standard.

Unfortunately, there is no treatment option available for hereditary deafness – it is the job of the dog owner to adapt to the loss of hearing. You may need to keep your dog in the house or confined to a leash because he may not be aware of dangers like moving cars. You might need to train your dog to respond to hand signals instead of verbal cues and the training process may take a little longer. Though there are additional challenges involved, deaf dogs can lead very long and happy lives with the right modifications.

## Urolithiasis or Hyperuricemia

As mentioned in a previous chapter, Dalmatians are prone to urinary tract infections that often lead to forming kidney or bladder stones. This condition is called Urolithiasis or Hyperuricemia. It is also a genetic defect of Dalmatians that is actually unique to their breed.

Fortunately, even if it is genetic, there are ways to avert serious health damage. Basically, the flaw in their urinary system is the inability to break down uric acid, which will always be present in digestion. The uric acid that is not urinated will eventually accumulate and form crystals that later turn to stones.

To avoid subjecting your dog to this condition, make sure you feed him a proper diet that is low in purines and heavily dense protein to aid, rather than burden, his digestive and urinary system. Just as important as his diet, make sure you provide him abundant water at all times and encourage him to hydrate himself often to help him urinate as much as possible in order to clean the potential build up. Regular check-ups for crystals are also recommended.

There is an ongoing study about this particular health concern which involves innovating treatment and management and it would be a good idea to discuss this with your veterinarian. Prevention is better than treatment especially in cases that you are already informed of the necessary precautions.

## Laryngeal paralysis

There is no known cause for this condition, which is another hereditary disease affecting Dalmatians. Unlike with hereditary deafness and urinary defect where the genes responsible for the problem are inescapable, breeding dogs that are afflicted with this condition is discouraged. Puppies born with this ailment may have difficulties in breathing and swallowing, may gag often and may have a weird sounding bark.

This disorder renders the larynx or voice box dysfunctional, wherein it cannot open or close properly. The larynx is one of the passageways of air so breathing becomes problematic with this disorder. If not treated accordingly, this could be fatal to your dog.

To detect this in your puppy, watch out for signs of hoarse barking, wheezing, and gagging. If he exhibits all symptoms bring him to your veterinarian right away and if he is diagnosed with the sickness, he will undergo surgery. Survival rate after surgery is high.

## *Preventing Illness with Vaccinations*

The best way to keep your Dalmatian healthy is to provide him with a nutritious and balanced diet. You also need to ensure that he gets proper veterinary care, and that includes routine vaccinations. Vaccinations will not protect your Dalmatian against nutritional deficiencies or inherited conditions, but they can help to protect him from certain communicable diseases like rabies, distemper, and parvovirus.

The vaccinations your Dalmatian needs may vary depending where you live since certain regions have a higher risk for certain diseases. Your vet will know which vaccinations your dog needs and when he needs them, but the vaccination schedule below will help you to keep track of when your Dalmatian needs to see the vet.

To give you an idea what kind of vaccinations your puppy will need, consult the vaccination schedule below:

| Vaccination Schedule for Dogs** | | | |
|---|---|---|---|
| **Vaccine** | **Doses** | **Age** | **Booster** |
| Rabies | 1 | 12 weeks | annual |
| Distemper | 3 | 6-16 weeks | 3 years |
| Parvovirus | 3 | 6-16 weeks | 3 years |
| Adenovirus | 3 | 6-16 weeks | 3 years |
| Parainfluenza | 3 | 6 weeks, 12-14 weeks | 3 years |
| Bordetella | 1 | 6 weeks | annual |
| Lyme Disease | 2 | 9, 13-14 weeks | annual |
| Leptospirosis | 2 | 12 and 16 weeks | annual |
| Canine Influenza | 2 | 6-8, 8-12 weeks | annual |

** Keep in mind that vaccine requirements may vary from one region to another. Only your vet will be able to tell you which vaccines are most important for the region where you live.

# Dalmatian Care Sheet

In reading this book, you have received a wealth of valuable information about the Dalmatian breed and caring for it as a pet. As you nurture your dog and your relationship with him, you will still find this book useful. But rather than flipping through the entire book, you can use this care sheet as your quick reference for the most basic information you might want to recall and review. This care sheet is a summary of all the useful information that a Dalmatian owner needs.

## 1.) Basic Dalmatian Information

**Pedigree**: exact origins unknown, but the earliest sightings are claimed to be in Croatia

**AKC Group**: Companion, Utility, Sporting Group

**Breed Size**: medium to large

**Height**: 20 – 22 inches (50 – 55 cm) for females and 22 – 24 inches (55 – 60 cm) for males

**Weight**: 48 – 55 pounds

**Coat Length**: short

**Coat Texture**: fine and dense

**Shedding**: extreme, 365 days a year

**Color**: white with black or liver spots

**Eyes**: brown, blue or both

**Nose**: black, liver, blue, dark gray

**Ears**: drop ears; set high, tapering to a rounded tip

**Tail**: topline extension, never docked, tapers to the tip, carried with a slight upward curve

**Temperament**: energetic, lively, playful, alert, intelligent, clingy, outgoing

**Strangers**: may greet them with enthusiastic jumping or be politely reserved

**Children**: generally good with children but should be supervised around young and small children

**Other Dogs**: generally good with other dogs and other animals if properly trained and socialized

**Training**: intelligent and very trainable

**Exercise Needs**: has an endless supply of energy; can never have enough exercise so provide as much as possible, should not be less than an hour a day

**Health Conditions**: deafness, hypopigmentation, epilepsy, urination complications that lead to kidney and bladder stones

**Lifespan**: average 10 to 13 years

**Nickname:** Dal

## 2.) Habitat Requirements

**Recommended Accessories**: crate, dog bed, fences/gates, food/water dishes, toys, collar, leash, harness, grooming supplies

**Collar and Harness**: sized by weight

**Grooming Supplies**: rubber curry brush

**Grooming Frequency**: brush daily, bathe once a week

**Energy Level**: extremely energetic and active

**Exercise Requirements**: as long and as frequent as your schedule allows you but not less than a daily 30-minute run or an hour walk

**Crate**: highly recommended

**Crate Size**: just large enough for dog to lie down and turn around comfortably

**Crate Extras**: lined with blanket or plush pet bed

**Food/Water**: stainless steel or ceramic bowls, clean daily

**Toys**: start with an assortment, see what the dog likes; include some mentally stimulating toys

**Exercise Ideas**: play games to give your dog extra exercise during the day; train your dog for various dog sports

*3.) Nutritional Needs*

**Nutritional Needs**: water, protein, carbohydrate, fats, vitamins, minerals

**Restrictions:** purine and heavily dense protein

**Calorie Needs**: varies by age, weight, and activity level

**Amount to Feed (puppy):** feed freely but consult recommendations on the package

**Amount to Feed (adult)**: consult recommendations on the package; calculated by weight

**Feeding Frequency**: two to three meals daily

**Important Ingredients**: fresh animal protein (chicken, beef, lamb, turkey, eggs), digestible carbohydrates (rice, oats, barley), animal fats

**Important Minerals**: calcium, phosphorus, potassium, magnesium, iron, copper and manganese

**Important Vitamins**: Vitamin A, Vitamin A, Vitamin B-12, Vitamin D, Vitamin C

**Look For**: AAFCO statement of nutritional adequacy; protein at top of ingredients list; no artificial flavors, dyes, preservatives

## 4.) Breeding Information

**Age of First Heat:** around 6 months (or earlier)

**Heat (Estrus) Cycle:** 14 to 21 days

**Frequency:** twice a year, every 6 to 7 months

**Breeding Age:** at least 2 years old, no more than 8

**Breeding Pair:** both good examples of the breed standard

**Time Between Litters:** at least one heat cycle, ideally one year

**Greatest Fertility:** 11 to 15 days into the cycle

**Gestation Period:** 61 to 65 days, average 63 days

**Pregnancy Detection:** possible after 21 days, best to wait 28 days before exam

**Feeding Pregnant Dogs:** maintain normal diet until week 5 or 6 then slightly increase rations

**Signs of Labor:** body temperature drops below normal 100° to 102°F (37.7° to 38.8°C), may be as low as 98°F (36.6°C); dog begins nesting in a dark, quiet place

**Contractions:** period of 10 minutes in waves of 3 to 5 followed by a period of rest

**Whelping:** puppies are born in 1/2 hour increments following 10 to 30 minutes of forceful straining

**Puppies:** born with eyes and ears closed; eyes open at 3 weeks, teeth develop at 10 weeks

**Litter Size:** 6 to 9 puppies

**Size at Birth:** about .75 – 2 pounds

**Weaning:** start offering puppy food soaked in water at 6 weeks; fully weaned by 8 weeks

**Socialization:** start as early as possible to prevent puppies from being nervous as an adult

# Index

## C

## D

# E

# F

# G

## H

## I

## K

## L

## M

# R

# S

# T

# References

"Dalmatian"AKC.
   <http://www.akc.org/dog-breeds/dalmatian/>

"Dalmatian" DogBreedInfo.
   <http://www.dogbreedinfo.com/dalmatian.htm>

"Dalmatian" Purina.
<http://www.purina.com.au/owning-a-dog/dog-breeds/Dalmatian>

"Dalmatian Dog" Wikipedia.
<https://en.wikipedia.org/wiki/Dalmatian_(dog)>

"Dalmatian Breed" PetMD.
<http://www.petmd.com/dog/breeds/c_dg_dalmatian>

"Dalmatian Breed" DogTime.
<http://dogtime.com/dog-breeds/dalmatian>

"Dalmatian Club of America" Dalmatian Club of America.
   <http://www.thedca.org/>

"Dalmatian Overview" Vetstreet.
   <http://www.vetstreet.com/dogs/dalmatian#overview>


"Diet Food and Treats" DalmatianBreed.
< http://dalmatianbreed.com/diet-food-and-treats/>

"Dog Training Methods" YourPureBredPuppy.
<http://www.yourpurebredpuppy.com/training/articles/dog-training-methods.html>

# Photo Credits

Introduction Photo by Klauskrumboeck via Pixabay.
<https://pixabay.com/en/sunrise-dalmatians-dog-forest-tree-1083936/>

Page 1 Photo by Lilaminze via Pixabay.
<https://pixabay.com/en/dalmatians-dog-pet-599681/>

Page 7 Photo by Miroslav Cacik via Wikimedia Commons.
<https://commons.wikimedia.org/wiki/File:Dalmatian_liver_stacked.jpg>

Page 9 Photo by Skeeze via Pixabay.
<https://pixabay.com/en/dalmatian-dog-portrait-pet-752509/>

Page 22 Photo by Unknown via Wikimedia Commons.
<https://commons.wikimedia.org/wiki/File:Dalmatian_dog.jpg>

Page 28 Photo by Skeeze via Pixabay.
<https://pixabay.com/en/dalmatian-canine-dog-pet-domestic-526959>

Page 38 Photo by Unknown via Wikimedia Commons.
<https://commons.wikimedia.org/wiki/File:Kim097.JPG>

Page 40 Photo by Wobogre via Pixabay.
<https://pixabay.com/en/dalmatians-dog-animal-pet-299588/>

Page 46 Photo by Huskyherz via Pixabay.
<https://pixabay.com/en/dog-dalmatians-pet-dog-breed-1020790/>

Page 48 Photo by Fgbdsfdsf via Pixabay.
<https://pixabay.com/en/dalmatian-dog-yawn-888517/>

Page 54 Photo by Heroyt via Pixabay.
<https://pixabay.com/en/dog-winter-dalmatian-path-snow-728719/>

Page 58 Photo by Heroyt via Pixabay.
<https://pixabay.com/en/dog-dalmatian-dog-ears-outdoors-740658/>

Page 64 Photo by Cocoparisienne via Pixabay.
<https://pixabay.com/en/dalmatians-dog-animal-head-765138/>

Page 71 Photo by Sam Hood via Wikimedia Commons.
<https://commons.wikimedia.org/wiki/File:SLNSW_50738_Champion_Dalmatian_dog_and_bitch.jpg>

Page 85 Photo by Skeeze via Pixabay.
<https://pixabay.com/en/dalmatian-dog-head-pet-canine-568645/>

Page 89 Photo by Tpsdave via Pixabay.
<https://pixabay.com/en/dalmatian-dog-canine-beautiful-82397/>

Page 95 Photo by Klauskrumboeck via Pixabay.
<https://pixabay.com/en/dalmatians-rock-sky-nature-1083910/>

Page 97 Photo by Lilaminze via Pixabay.
<https://pixabay.com/en/dog-dalmatians-animals-595031/>

Feeding Baby
Cynthia Cherry
978-1941070000

Axolotl
Lolly Brown
978-0989658430

Dysautonomia, POTS
Syndrome
Frederick Earlstein
978-0989658485

Degenerative Disc
Disease Explained
Frederick Earlstein
978-0989658485

Sinusitis, Hay Fever,
Allergic Rhinitis Explained
Frederick Earlstein
978-1941070024

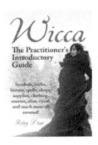

Wicca
Riley Star
978-1941070130

Zombie Apocalypse
Rex Cutty
978-1941070154

Capybara
Lolly Brown
978-1941070062

Eels As Pets
Lolly Brown
978-1941070167

Scabies and Lice Explained
Frederick Earlstein
978-1941070017

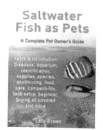

Saltwater Fish As Pets
Lolly Brown
978-0989658461

Torticollis Explained
Frederick Earlstein
978-1941070055

Kennel Cough
Lolly Brown
978-0989658409

Physiotherapist, Physical
Therapist
Christopher Wright
978-0989658492

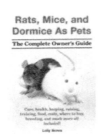

Rats, Mice, and Dormice
As Pets
Lolly Brown
978-1941070079

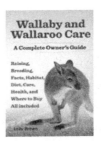

Wallaby and Wallaroo Care
Lolly Brown
978-1941070031

Bodybuilding Supplements
Explained
Jon Shelton
978-1941070239

Demonology
Riley Star
978-19401070314

Pigeon Racing
Lolly Brown
978-1941070307

Dwarf Hamster
Lolly Brown
978-1941070390

Cryptozoology
Rex Cutty
978-1941070406

Eye Strain
Frederick Earlstein
978-1941070369

Inez The Miniature Elephant
Asher Ray
978-1941070353

Vampire Apocalypse
Rex Cutty
978-1941070321